Saturn

by Gregory L. Vogt

Consultant:
Ralph Winrich
Aerospace Education Specialist
for NASA

Bridgestone Books
an imprint of Capstone Press
Mankato, Minnesota

Bridgestone Books are published by Capstone Press
151 Good Counsel Drive, P.O. Box 669, Mankato, Minnesota 56002
http://www.capstone-press.com

Library of Congress Cataloging-in-Publication Data
Vogt, Gregory.
    Saturn/by Gregory L. Vogt.
    p. cm.—(The galaxy)
    Includes bibliographical references and index.
    Summary: Discusses the orbit, atmosphere, rings, moons, surface features, exploration,
and other aspects of the planet Saturn.
    ISBN 0-7368-0515-X
    1. Saturn (Planet)—Juvenile literature. [1. Saturn (Planet).] I. Title. II. Series.
QB671 .V643 2000
523.46—dc21   99-86980

Editorial Credits
Erika Mikkelson, editor; Timothy Halldin, cover designer and illustrator;
    Kimberly Danger and Jodi Theisen, photo researchers

Photo Credits
Astronomical Society of the Pacific/NASA, 6, 10, 16, 18
NASA, cover, 1, 8, 12, 14, 20

1 2 3 4 5 6   05 04 03 02 01 00

Table of Contents

Relative size of the Sun and the planets

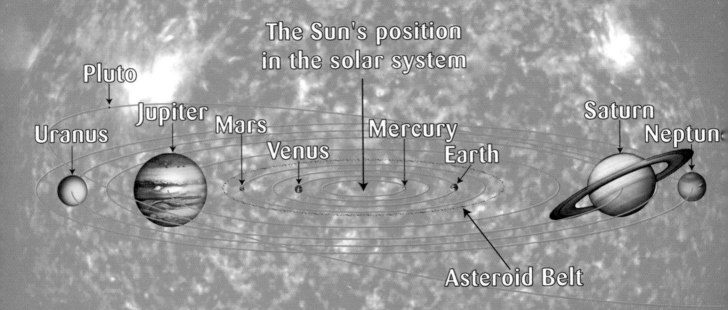

Pluto

Uranus

Jupiter

Mars

Venus

The Sun's position in the solar system

Mercury

Earth

Saturn

Neptun

Asteroid Belt

The Sun

Saturn is a planet in the solar system. The Sun is the center of the solar system. Planets, asteroids, and comets travel around the Sun. Saturn is the sixth planet from the Sun.

The four planets closest to the Sun are made of rock. They are Mercury, Venus, Earth, and Mars. Jupiter, Saturn, Uranus, and Neptune are farther from the Sun. These giant planets are made of gases. Pluto is the last planet. Rock and ice make up Pluto.

Through a telescope, Saturn is easy to recognize. Thousands of rings circle the planet. Saturn has larger rings than any other planet in the solar system.

This illustration compares the sizes of the planets and the Sun. Saturn is the second largest planet in the solar system. The blue lines show the orbits of the planets. Thousands of asteroids move around the Sun. The asteroid belt is between the orbits of Mars and Jupiter.

FAST FACTS

	Saturn	Earth
Diameter:	74,899 miles (120,535 kilometers)	7,927 miles (12,756 kilometers)
Average distance from the Sun:	888 million miles (1,429 million kilometers)	93 million miles (150 million kilometers)
Revolution period:	29 years, 6 months	365 days, 6 hours
Rotation period:	10 hours, 40 minutes	23 hours, 56 minutes
Moons:	18	1

Saturn is the second largest planet in the solar system. Only Saturn's nearest neighbor, Jupiter, is larger. Saturn is 74,899 miles (120,535 kilometers) wide. The planet is almost 10 times wider than Earth.

Thousands of rings orbit Saturn. From Earth, the rings look solid. Astronomers once believed that Saturn was the only planet with rings. In 1977, they discovered that Uranus also has rings. Astronomers soon learned that rings circle all the giant planets. Only Saturn's rings are bright enough to be seen from Earth.

Saturn is the only planet in the solar system that is less dense than water. Saturn is not heavy compared to its size. It would float if there were an ocean big enough to hold it.

The space probe *Voyager 2* took this photograph of Saturn. It shows Saturn, its rings, and three of its inner moons.

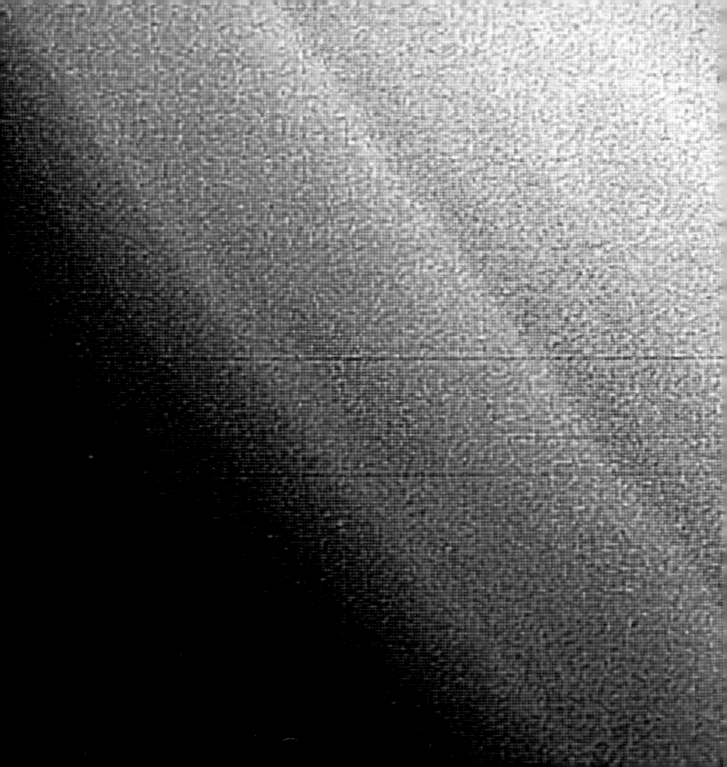

Atmosphere

A mixture of gases called an atmosphere surrounds most planets. Saturn's atmosphere is made of hydrogen and helium gases. The planet's atmosphere also has small amounts of methane and ethane.

Clouds in Saturn's atmosphere form light-colored bands around the planet. The bands are clouds in Saturn's atmosphere. Strong winds move the clouds around the planet at speeds up to 1,100 miles (1,800 kilometers) per hour. The wind stretches the clouds into bands. Storms sometimes swirl in the bands like whirlpools.

Saturn is a very cold planet. The temperature in its upper atmosphere is minus 287 degrees Fahrenheit (minus 177 degrees Celsius). Little of the Sun's heat reaches Saturn. The planet is 888 million miles (1,429 million kilometers) from the Sun. The distance is more than nine times farther from the Sun than Earth. Life as we know it cannot exist in Saturn's cold weather.

The colors in this photograph show Saturn's atmosphere. The red and blue areas are clouds.

This symbol represents Saturn. All planets except Earth are named for characters in Greek or Roman myths. In these ancient stories, Saturn was the Roman god of agriculture.

Revolution and Rotation

Saturn and the other planets move around the Sun in a path called an orbit. Saturn makes one revolution around the Sun every 29 years and 6 months. Earth orbits the Sun every 365 days and 6 hours. One year on Saturn would be nearly 11,000 Earth days long.

Astronomers cannot see Saturn's rings at certain points in the planet's orbit. Saturn is tilted. A shadow falls on part of the rings when the Sun's light hits the planet.

Saturn spins as it orbits the Sun. The planet makes one rotation every 10 hours and 40 minutes. Saturn's fast rotation causes the planet to appear slightly flattened. Only Jupiter rotates faster than Saturn. Jupiter rotates once every 9 hours and 55 minutes.

Saturn's tilt causes its shadow to cover a part of the rings.

The Hubble Space Telescope photographed a storm on Saturn in 1994. The storm appears as a white arrowhead near Saturn's equator. *Voyager 1* and *Voyager 2* took the photographs below. The bright oval in the lower right of both photos is a giant storm.

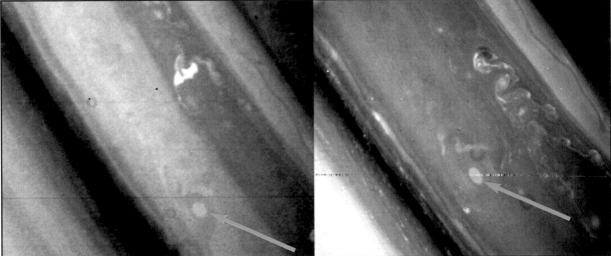

Voyager 1 photograph

Voyager 2 photograph

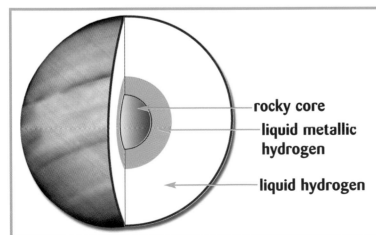

rocky core

liquid metallic hydrogen

liquid hydrogen

At the center of Saturn is a rocky core. A layer of liquid metallic hydrogen surrounds the core. Above that layer is a layer of liquid hydrogen. Storms form in Saturn's atmosphere, which lies above the liquid hydrogen.

Saturn's atmosphere is usually calm. High-speed winds move clouds smoothly around the planet. Astronomers have seen three major storms on Saturn.

Scientists saw the first storm on Saturn in 1930. A larger storm appeared in 1990. In 1994, astronomers noticed a much bigger storm brewing. Scientists call the storm the Great White Spot.

The storm appeared along Saturn's middle. It looked like a white arrowhead. The storm grew in size until it was larger than Earth. Warm gases deep inside the atmosphere moved upward. Ammonia gas in the clouds froze when it reached the upper atmosphere. The ammonia ice crystals gave the storm clouds a white color.

Rings

Galileo Galilei was the first astronomer to study Saturn through a telescope. Galileo lived in Italy in the 1600s. He saw Saturn's rings but did not know what they were. He thought the rings looked like ears. Galileo's telescope was not powerful enough to see the rings clearly.

Today, scientists have learned that Saturn has thousands of rings. Astronomers call them ringlets. The innermost ringlets are about 4,350 miles (7,000 kilometers) away from Saturn's clouds. The outermost ringlets are about 46,000 miles (74,000 kilometers) from the planet.

Saturn's rings probably formed when meteorites struck the planet's moons. The meteorites blasted ice and rock away from the moons. Small pieces spread out and formed rings around Saturn. The average pieces range from the size of a marble to the size of a basketball.

Scientists used computers to add colors to this image. This image shows more than 60 bright and dark ringlets.

Saturn has 18 known moons. Saturn's moons are made of rock and ice.

Titan is Saturn's largest moon. It is 3,200 miles (5,150 kilometers) wide. Titan is three times larger than Rhea, the next largest moon. Saturn's moons often are each less than 950 miles (1,530 kilometers) across. Five of the planet's moons are less than 20 miles (32 kilometers) wide.

Each of Saturn's moons looks different. Enceladus has cracks and valleys. Mimas has a giant crater. A meteorite struck Mimas and formed a large hole in its surface. A mountain formed in the middle of the crater. Iapetus is half light in color and half dark. Hyperion is a bumpy moon. Meteorites probably knocked off pieces of Hyperion.

A meteorite formed a giant crater on the surface of Mimas.

Titan

Saturn's moon Titan is the second largest moon in the solar system. Only Jupiter's bright moon, Ganymede, is bigger. Both moons are larger than the planet Mercury.

Titan is the only moon in the solar system with a thick atmosphere. The atmosphere is mainly nitrogen gas and is about 200 miles (320 kilometers) thick. Titan's atmosphere is so thick that astronomers have never seen its surface. Astronomers think Titan is made of rock and ice.

Titan's atmosphere interests astronomers who study Earth. The moon's atmosphere may be similar to Earth's atmosphere billions of years ago. Studying Titan could lead to clues about Earth's past.

Astronomers may learn more about Titan in the near future. The *Cassini* space probe is on its way to Saturn. *Cassini* will gather information about Titan's atmosphere.

Titan's clouds hide the moon's surface. *Voyager 1* took this photograph of the edge of Titan.

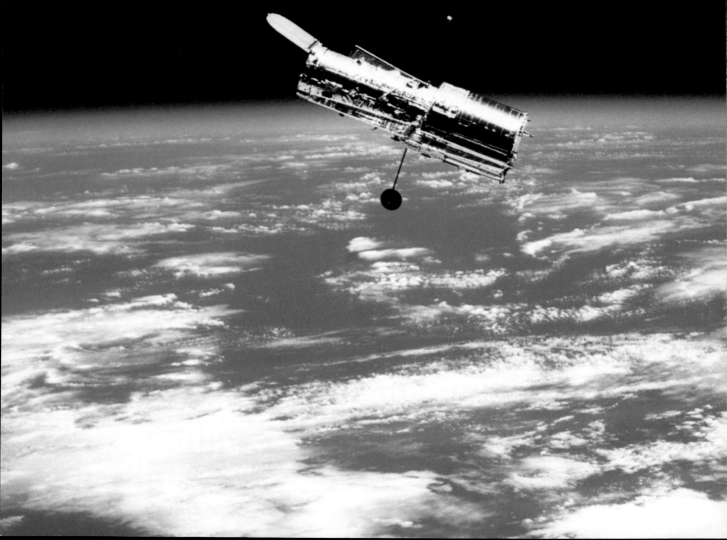

In the 1970s, scientists sent three space probes to study Saturn. *Pioneer 11* arrived first in 1979. The other two space probes, *Voyager 1* and *Voyager 2*, arrived in the early 1980s. Each of the space probes took a few weeks to fly past Saturn.

The space probes carried cameras. The probes sent pictures to Earth through radio waves. Computer screens displayed the pictures. Since 1979, astronomers have learned about Saturn by studying the pictures.

In 1990, scientists launched the Hubble Space Telescope. This large telescope orbits Earth. Scientists use the Hubble to take pictures of objects in space. The Hubble often takes pictures of Saturn.

The *Cassini* space probe is expected to reach Saturn in 2004. *Cassini* will take more than 500,000 pictures of Saturn, its rings, and Titan.

The Hubble Space Telescope orbits Earth. Scientists use the telescope to take photographs of Saturn and other objects in space.

Hands On: Saturn's Rings

Saturn's rings circle the planet. Through a telescope, the rings do not look circular. Instead, they look like flattened circles. Find out why they look this way.

What You Need

Modeling clay
Plastic knife
Compact disc
Friend to help you

What You Do

1. Form the modeling clay into a ball. The ball should be one inch (2.5 centimeters) in diameter. Cut the ball in half. Place one half on each side of the CD.
2. Stand about 10 feet (3 meters) away from your friend.
3. Ask your friend to hold the CD so you can see its flat surface. Pretend the CD is Saturn's rings. The rings should look like a circle.
4. Ask your friend to slowly tilt the CD. Stop when the CD is tilted halfway. This is the way the rings look from Earth.
5. Ask your friend to tilt the CD until it is horizontal. Sometimes we see the edges of Saturn's rings. Do you think they would be easy to see?
6. Trade places with your friend and repeat steps 3-5.

Words to Know

astronomer (uh-STRON-uh-mer)—a person who studies the planets, stars, and space

atmosphere (AT-muhss-feehr)—the mixture of gases that surrounds some planets

comet (KOM-it)—a ball of rock and ice that orbits the Sun

meteorite (MEE-tee-ur-rite)—a piece of space rock that strikes a planet or a moon

orbit (OR-bit)—the path of an object as it travels around another object in space

revolution (rev-uh-LOO-shuhn)—the movement of one object around another object

ring (RING)—a band of rock and dust orbiting a planet

ringlet (RING-let)—a small ring orbiting Saturn

rotation (roh-TAY-shuhn)—one complete spin of an object in space

space probe (SPAYSS PROHB)—a spacecraft that travels to the planets and outer space

Read More

Brimner, Larry Dane. *Saturn.* A True Book. New York: Children's Press, 1999.

Murray, Peter. *Saturn.* Chanhassen, Minn.: Child's World, 1998.

Simon, Seymour. *Our Solar System.* New York: William Morrow, 1998.

Useful Addresses

Canadian Space Agency
6767 Route de l'Aéroport
Saint-Hubert, QC J3Y 8Y9
Canada

NASA Headquarters
Washington, DC 20546-0001

The Planetary Society
65 Catalina Avenue
Pasadena, CA 91106-2301

Internet Sites

Canadian Space Agency-Kidspace
http://www.space.gc.ca/kidspace/index.html

The Nine Planets
http://www.tcsn.net/afiner

Index